100
Multicultural
PROVERBS

This book is dedicated to innovative educators
and leaders
who shift their paradigm and power to:
see not only with their eyes, but also with their
ears, head, mouth, and heart;
hear not only with their ears, but also with their
eyes, head, mouth, and heart;
talk not only with their mouth, but also with
their eyes, ears, head, and heart;
think not only with their head, but also with
their eyes, ears, heart, and mouth;
care not only with their heart, but also with
their eyes, ears, head, and mouth.

100
Multicultural
PROVERBS

Inspirational Affirmations for Educators

Festus E. Obiakor

Foreword by Jacob U. Gordon
Afterword by William B. Harvey

CORWIN PRESS
A SAGE Company
Thousand Oaks, CA 91320

For information:

Corwin Press	SAGE India Pvt. Ltd.
A SAGE Company	B 1/I 1 Mohan Cooperative
2455 Teller Road	Industrial Area
Thousand Oaks,	Mathura Road, New Delhi 110 044
California 91320	India
www.corwinpress.com	
SAGE Ltd.	SAGE Asia-Pacific Pte. Ltd.
1 Oliver's Yard	33 Pekin Street #02–01
55 City Road	Far East Square
London EC1Y 1SP	Singapore 048763
United Kingdom	

Printed in the United States of America.

Library of Congress Cataloging-in-Publication Data

Obiakor, Festus E.
100 multicultural proverbs : inspirational affirmations for educators / Festus E. Obiakor.
    p. cm.
Includes bibliographical references and index.
ISBN 978-1-4129-5779-3 (cloth)
ISBN 978-1-4129-5780-9 (pbk.)
    1. Proverbs. 2. Education—Quotations, maxims, etc.
3. Inspiration—Quotations, maxims, etc. I. Title. II. Title: One hundred multicultural proverbs.

PN6405.O25 2008
398.9—dc22   2007031653

This book is printed on acid-free paper.

07   08   09   10   11   10   9   8   7   6   5   4   3   2   1

Acquisitions Editor:	Allyson P. Sharp
Editorial Assistant:	David Andrew Gray
Production Editor:	Veronica Stapleton
Typesetter:	C&M Digitals (P) Ltd.
Proofreader:	Dorothy Hoffman
Cover Designer:	Lisa Miller

Contents

CHAPTER TWO: PROVERBS THAT TEACH
COLLABORATION AND CONSULTATION   **26**

CHAPTER THREE: PROVERBS THAT
TEACH SPIRITUALITY   51

CHAPTER FOUR: PROVERBS THAT TEACH
OTHER LIFE LESSONS   **76**

Foreword

S ince the dawn of civilization, the human race has endeavored to communicate through thousands of languages and dialects, some of which have disappeared for various reasons. It is estimated that the continent of Africa alone has more than eight hundred distinct languages and dialects. Similarly, other continents boast of widely varied languages and dialects. While the invention of writing and modern technology has helped to advance various communication media, some traditional methods continue to be widely used. One of these sharing wisdom styles is the use of proverbs. This method of sharing wisdom is as old as the history of humanity.

Many countries and their peoples have had their shares of inventions. Consider these examples. One of the earliest forms of literacy in the world, hieroglyphic writing, was invented in ancient Egypt around 3000 BC. In the south of Egypt, the Kushitic civilization had its own form of writing five centuries or more before the birth of Christ. In neighboring Ethiopia, Ge'ez, the classical language of ancient Axum, was expressed in written form by the fourth century AD. Apparently other literary traditions existed in Western and non-Western languages, such as English, French, Chinese, and Arabic. These traditions have continued to use proverbs in some way or fashion; many have cross-germinated and crossed boundaries in different parts of the world.

The word "proverb" has been defined by the *Merriam-Webster's Collegiate Dictionary, 11th ed.,* 2003, as a "brief popular epigram or maxim" (see the Merriam-Webster Dictionary). In *100 Multicultural Proverbs: Inspirational Affirmations for Educators,* Professor Festus Obiakor provides more clarity to the meaning of proverb. Although the universality of the use of proverbs has been well documented, this book is second to none. Professor Obiakor gives readers more than a tour of the world's proverbs and their applications. His selection of proverbs and the conceptual framework for the book are, to say the least, powerful.

Equally impressive and effective are his brief interpretations and prescriptions for the appropriate use of these proverbs for those involved in education, leadership, and service provision.

100 Multicultural Proverbs is a book that represents a rich, lively, and positive commentary on our global cultures. It is a masterpiece that will appeal to the widest audiences. It is a book that stimulates further exploration into proverbs as a critical source of communication. Essential for every bookshelf, this book should be required reading for all ages, present and future generations. Professor Obiakor's perceptive guidance to all highlights why this book should be a necessity to those in Education, Multicultural Education, African Studies, Global Studies, Linguistics, International Education, International Relations, and Human Relations. My hope is that educators and leaders will creatively use this book in resolving the toughest human problems as they build communities in this age of change.

Jacob U. Gordon, PhD, LLD
Professor Emeritus, African and African American Studies
University of Kansas

REFERENCE

Merriam-Webster's Collegiate Dictionary, 11th ed., 2003.

Publisher's Note: While Corwin Press normally strives for inclusive language in referring to a person of nonspecified gender, the proverbs in this book date back to older times and other cultures. Readers should be aware that any mention of "he" or "him" may also include females.

Preface

P roverbs are an important part of life, and they are intertwined with the sociocultural and political webs of the world's peoples. They depict and unveil generational tradition, consistency, continuity, wisdom, power, pride, humility, imperfection, prejudice, spirituality, and religiosity. The connectivity of these constructs highlights the humanity that is attached to proverbs. This humanity transcends generational values. Growing up in Nigeria, West Africa, I learned very early from my father and grandfather that *proverbs constitute the oil with which we eat our words.* As a member of the Igbo tribe, I was taught that *proverbs are understood by the wise, but the fool turns his neck into the bush.* To a large measure, proverbs provide deeper philosophical meanings and simplified progressive explications of complex principles, situations, events, and activities. They massage messages and add succinctness to the daily interactive and multicultural lives of peoples and communities. In addition, they portray a true picture of the originality of the world's peoples and demonstrate authentic valuing of oral traditions and verbalizations. In more ways than one, proverbs expose innermost dialogue and discourse as a part of the modus vivendi of our multicultural and universal world. In intricate and exquisite conversations, they have become the "icing on the cake" in many Western and non-Western societies, cultures, and communities. In short, proverbs transcend national, tribal, cultural, linguistic, and religious boundaries.

I began to think about writing *100 Multicultural Proverbs: Inspirational Affirmations for Educators* a few years ago when former First Lady and now-current Senator Hillary Rodham Clinton (1996) popularized the African proverb *It takes a village to raise a child* through her best-selling book. In my research, I found proverbs from varied and fascinating tribes and languages (e.g., Arabic, Chinese, Edo,

Farsi, Hausa, Hebrew, Igbo, Italian, Yoruba, Kiswahili, Macedonian, Navajo, Patua, Portuguese, Spanish, Xhosa, and Zulu, among others) across the world. With some assistance, I found powerful and historic proverbs from some African nations (e.g., Benin, Cameroon, Egypt, Ethiopia, Ghana, Guinea, Kenya, Madagascar, Mali, Nigeria, Senegal, Sierra Leone, Somalia, South Africa, Sudan, Tanzania, Uganda, and Zaire); some Caribbean nations (e.g., Barbados, Jamaica, and Trinidad); some Latin American nations (e.g., Brazil, Chili, Cuba, Mexico, and Venezuela); and some Western and non-Western nations (e.g., Canada, China, England, India, Israel, Italy, France, Macedonia, Pakistan, Russia, and Turkey). It was interesting to find that in different continents, countries, tribes, and communities some proverbs are similar in wordings, meanings, and contexts. It also became clear that proverbs are embedded in many, if not all, traditional and nontraditional religious faiths (e.g., Baptist, Buddhist, Catholic, Episcopal, Jewish, Mormon, Muslim, and many more).

Many indigenous and traditional peoples have used proverbs for community collaboration, consultation, and cooperation; among these peoples, the elders preside over discussions and share their generational ideals with the youth and young children. As a result, these elders infuse and build a kind of cultural steadiness or continuity that has stood the test of time. Interestingly, these ideals have begun to infiltrate our global values and world scenes. My belief is that the complexity of the world's problems calls for new ways of thinking, discussing, sharing, teaching, and learning. In addition, I am convinced that we need to go back to those traditional and multicultural ways of using words, sharing ideas, and solving problems to build and sustain communities. Without doubt, proverbs are words that have proven to be powerful to the sacred existence of human beings! Clearly, they have tribal, national, and universal implications for today's changing world.

In *100 Multicultural Proverbs,* I present and explain proverbs from different continents, countries, tribes, religions, languages, communities, and peoples. As we can see, these proverbs expose different and similar voices on how best to communicate with others and build communities. We know that technology has helped to make the world a smaller place—people now know instantly what is happening in other places. News, goods, and people travel from place to place, and we have external burdens and influences that impinge upon how we live and interact with each other. For example, the integration of immigrant minorities into the fabric of U.S. society brings to light external imperatives for educators, service providers, and leaders struggling to change their ways of thinking, doing, learning, teaching, and leading. Clearly, the paradigms and powers are shifting at a startling rate in our society—we can and must learn from each other to enhance human life. In writing this book, I found that most proverbs have pertinent connection to the development of human potential, individual and collective responsibility, multicultural collaboration and consultation, spiritual fortitude, and strengths from life's universal lessons.

100 Multicultural Proverbs has four chapters. Chapter One contains proverbs that teach self-responsibility; Chapter Two has proverbs that teach collaboration and consultation; Chapter Three contains proverbs that teach spirituality; and Chapter Four contains proverbs that teach other life lessons. Though this book is written for educators and leaders, it is also written for service providers and professionals of all kinds. It should be on the reading list of anyone who works with other people. Hopefully, people involved in leadership training will find it useful. As it appears, this book can be used as a major or supplementary text for undergraduate and graduate courses in Counseling, Psychology, Philosophy, Education, Multicultural Education, African/African American Studies, Africology, Educational Leadership, Anthropology, World Literature, Literacy, Foreign Language, International Studies, and Global Studies.

This book would not have been successful without the support of family and friends. My heartfelt thanks go to my wife, Pauline, and children, Charles, Gina, Kristen, and Alicia, for their support and patience during this book project. I want to especially thank Dr. Jacob Gordon, Professor Emeritus of the University of Kansas, for sharing his collection of proverbs with me and for writing the Foreword of this book. In addition, my sincere thanks go to Dr. Bill Harvey, Vice President for Diversity and Equity Services, University of Virginia, for writing the Afterword of this book. I am grateful to many individuals, especially Dr. Michael Afolayan, Dr. Mesut Akdere, Dr. Osman Alawiye, Dr. Innocent Aluka, Dr. Idayatou Anjorin, Rev. Father Felix Anyikwa, Dr. Samuel Awe, Dr. Anthony Azenabor, Ms. Djanabou Balde, Dr. Katerina Belazelkoska, Dr. Simone Conceição, Dr. Pat Garvey, Mr. Pete Gonzales, Dr. Patrick Grant, Dr. Zandile Nkabinde, Mr. Ugo Okoro, Dr. Gathogo Mukuria, Dr. Anthony Rotatori, Dr. Paul Sagal, Dr. Timothy Smith, Mr. Chinedu L. Tabugbo, Mr. Koreissi Tall, Mr. Godwin Ubayionwu, and Mr. Donatus Udensi for sharing their collection of proverbs with me. For instance, in my February 2007 visit to

Indiana University–Purdue University at Fort Wayne, Indiana, I talked with Dr. Pat Garvey, a professor and former school superintendent who recalled using proverbs like *Your dilemma is not my emergency* and *There is no hope for a better past* to motivate and humorously challenge his staff and colleagues as he solved minor irritating problems, resolved serious conflicts, and stabilized his organizational community. Similarly, in my March 2007 visit to Brigham Young University, Provo, Utah, I spoke with Dr. Timothy Smith, a professor and Mormon Bishop, who indicated his appreciation for the ecumenical nature of proverbs and how "like images and stories, they speak to the soul." My interactions with Dr. Garvey and Dr. Smith demonstrate that proverbs powerfully excite the positive spirits of education, leadership, and life. I want to acknowledge my colleague, Dr. Faith Crampton, who got so inspired by my frequent conversational use of proverbs that she suggested that I write a book on proverbs. Finally, my special thanks go to Dr. Luciana Ugrina of the Word Processing Department of the School of Education, University of Wisconsin–Milwaukee, for sharing some spiritual proverbs with me and for her dedicated support in this work.

F. E. O.

REFERENCE

Clinton, H. R. (1996). *It takes a village and other lessons children teach us.* New York: Simon & Schuster.

About the Author

 Festus E. Obiakor, PhD, is Professor and Coordinator of Graduate Programs in the Department of Exceptional Education at the University of Wisconsin–Milwaukee. His research interests include multicultural psychology and special education, self-concept development, crisis intervention, educational reform, and comparative/international education. He is a renowned scholar with more than 150 publications, including books and journal articles. He serves on the editorial boards of many refereed journals, including *Multiple Voices* and *Multicultural Learning and Teaching*—he currently serves as co-editor of both journals. He has presented papers at national and international levels. In addition, he is a frequent speaker on college campuses; for example, he has served as an Invited/Visiting Scholar at Frostburg State University, Marquette University, Hendrix College, St. Xavier University of Chicago, Indiana University of Pennsylvania, Hampton University, Portland State University, the University of Georgia, West Virginia University, Eastern Illinois University, University of North Texas, Brigham Young University, Illinois State University, Tennessee State University, Morgan State University, Abilene Christian University, Grambling State University, and Indiana University–Purdue University.

CHAPTER ONE

Proverbs That Teach Self-Responsibility

೦೩ ಜಾ

> *PROVERB #1: If everyone loves you, you will not know who poisoned you.*

UNDERLYING EDUCATIONAL PRINCIPLES

It is important for someone to be principled and disciplined in decision making. In education and in life, people make tough decisions that are sometimes unpopular. Good leaders are frequently respected for their ability to move the system or organization forward, even when their decisions are not popular. This does not, however, mean that great education and leadership must be ruthless and careless. It means that people must do what is right, even when it is unpopular, as long as the society will be advanced by their actions.

೦೩ ಜಾ

> # PROVERB #2: *If you tell a tree that you will kill it, it will stand still and look at you; but if you tell a human being that you will kill him, the tendency will be for him to find safety in flight or fight back.*

UNDERLYING EDUCATIONAL PRINCIPLES

The difference between a tree and a human being is that the latter has the brain to think of survival strategies. Good educators and leaders think through situations before they get out of hand. Problems cannot solve themselves—prudent educators and leaders solve them. As a result, there must be true love and goodness in what we say and do. Our actions can have far-reaching impacts on fellow humans whether in our classrooms or organizations.

> ## PROVERB #3: The rat that joins the lizard to get wet in the rain will not be dry like the lizard when it stops raining.

UNDERLYING EDUCATIONAL PRINCIPLES

It is important that people understand their roles and responsibilities. You do not do something because someone else has done it. As educators and leaders, we must be responsible as we teach our students and colleagues how not to imitate counterproductive behaviors. Everyone must be accountable for the organization or system to work. To increase the potential for accountability, people must talk and listen to each other. Mistakes are frequently prevented where there are diagnostic (pre-action), formative (during action), and summative (end of action) accountabilities.

> ## PROVERB #4: *What you're looking for is what you will get.*

UNDERLYING EDUCATIONAL PRINCIPLES

With personal determination and hard work, individuals achieve their goals. As educators, we must help students to set goals and develop accurate self-knowledge, self-valuation, and self-responsibility. Good leaders tap into personal resiliency and determination in achieving life's goals. Our success and failures are based on our efforts and abilities to change.

PROVERB #5: What a person does is in his heart.

UNDERLYING EDUCATIONAL PRINCIPLES

There are differences between words and actions. What we do reflects our heart and who we are. Educators and leaders cannot divorce themselves from their actions—their actions reflect who they are and where their hearts are. As a result, they must understand that their actions have far-reaching consequences. Remember, we cannot read a person's heart; but what one does might tell us more about him.

> ## PROVERB #6: If you've not reached where you're going, you should keep going.

UNDERLYING EDUCATIONAL PRINCIPLES

Persistence and resiliency are important survival ingredients. As educators and leaders, we must be principled and committed to our personal goals and objectives. In addition, we must try to achieve them in a much more visionary method. It is not enough that one is going somewhere; it is what he will do when he gets there that is critical. Clearly, we are all travelers toward certain destinations or decisions.

PROVERB #7: Eneke the Bird noted that since men have learned to shoot without missing, it has learned to fly without perching.

UNDERLYING EDUCATIONAL PRINCIPLES

We must be tactful in what we do since every action has a reaction. We all have emotions, yet we must be careful in how we use them. Educators and leaders must be mindful about the ramifications of their actions because they frequently have some positive or negative ripple effects. People's intentions can be misread and misinterpreted. As a result, it behooves us to be prudent and caring as we interact with people.

PROVERB #8: Your intelligence is your handbag, and you carry it wherever you go.

UNDERLYING EDUCATIONAL PRINCIPLES

People do not all think alike. We have our own individual strengths or weaknesses, and we must acknowledge them. Also, group members do not all think in the same way. As educators, we cannot afford to judge a group or make a group comparison on the basis of intelligence scores. Good leaders rely on multidimensional assessment procedures to make fundamental decisions about people, events, and situations.

> # PROVERB #9: *When a young man washes his hands properly, he can eat with the kings.*

UNDERLYING EDUCATIONAL PRINCIPLES

Youthful exuberance is not always a good excuse. Self-responsibility and personal dedications are keys to success. There are young people with vision and we must encourage them. Many young people have exemplified themselves as leaders. For example, Dr. Martin Luther King, Jr., started very early to advocate for civil rights. Bill Gates, today's richest man in the world, started very early to exemplify himself as a technologically creative person. As a result, we must provide educational and leadership opportunities to young people. In addition, we must value and reward their hard work and actively listen to them, especially when they have proven themselves.

PROVERB #10: *The lizard that fell from the Iroko tree said that if you do not praise it, it will praise itself.*

UNDERLYING EDUCATIONAL PRINCIPLES

We cannot build resiliency without acknowledging self-worth and self-responsibility. The job of educators or leaders is to develop self-knowledge, self-esteem, and self-ideal in those with whom they come in contact. Some educators and leaders tend to devalue their students or team members. This behavior can be counterproductive because it disrupts individual or group ability to optimize potential. Good educators and leaders are cheerleaders. But when they cannot deliver, individuals must be their own cheerleaders for mental sanity and emotional stability.

PROVERB #11: *The person who blows the flute must sometimes wipe his mouth.*

UNDERLYING EDUCATIONAL PRINCIPLES

Whatever we do begins with the self. In order to build other people's self-concepts, we must accurately know who we are. Educators and leaders must value themselves before they value others. However, they must be cautious that their "selves" do not consume them as they interact with their students, clients, and cohorts. The absolute pursuit of the "self" could lead to nepotism, tribalism, and favoritism. Sometimes, we take care of our own at the expense of helping others in the community. In the process, educators and leaders must value or reward themselves but not at the expense of honesty and integrity.

PROVERB #12: The dog does not chew the bone that is hanging around its neck.

UNDERLYING EDUCATIONAL PRINCIPLES

We have power to do different things—we can do the right thing or the wrong thing. However, with freedom comes self-responsibility. Educators and leaders must be careful about what to do with their powers. They must understand that they are custodians of the well-being of their students, clients, colleagues, and coworkers. In addition, they must not abuse their powers as they work and relate with others similar to or different from them.

> *PROVERB #13: If you do not allow people to know what your size is, you will be carried beyond your father's compound.*

UNDERLYING EDUCATIONAL PRINCIPLES

We must know our self-worth—we have the negative tendency to misinterpret who we are, what we love, and what we do. These kinds of understanding frequently prevent poor judgments, negative conclusions, and prejudicial actions. Educators and leaders must make their principles, goals, and objectives known in their teachings, interactions, and activities. They must be honest with themselves as they analyze and evaluate their personal and systemic strengths, weaknesses, and limitations. There is honor in speaking the truth even when it hurts.

> ## PROVERB #14: If you pull a tree and it pulls you back, you should leave it alone.

UNDERLYING EDUCATIONAL PRINCIPLES

In life, we have personal and situational differences. Some things are beyond remediation even when we try our very best to handle them. As humans, we need to know when to take our losses and move on. One way to solve problems is to exhaust all avenues. However, it is also important to know when those avenues are exhausted. Our goal must always be to do the best we can. As educators and leaders, we need to know our boundaries and when we have overstepped those boundaries. We must know as individuals when to say "Yes" or "No" in whatever we do—it is our personal decision that is dependent on situational variables.

PROVERB #15: *If one is not careful, what destroyed his father might destroy him.*

UNDERLYING EDUCATIONAL PRINCIPLES

Personal responsibility must prevail in all that we do. We have roles to play in redirecting our future—we cannot continue to blame our past. We can prevent negative experiences by addressing past mistakes as we look toward the future. Educators and leaders cannot succeed until they resolve conflicts and deal with past negative situations. They can set new goals and adopt new objectives to achieve them. When they fail to be careful about past mistakes, the tendency is for them to repeat them. They must disrupt the circle of failure and institute the circle of success if they want their big ideas to materialize.

PROVERB #16: As you make your bed so will you lie on it.

UNDERLYING EDUCATIONAL PRINCIPLES

We are responsible for our own actions, and any problem we leave unsolved will continue to remain a problem until we solve it. We cannot continue to defer our problems to other people; at some point in life, we must accept them as our creation. As educators and leaders, we have phenomenal roles to play in creating our problems and solutions. It is crucial that we understand that we are the architects of our future. Consequently, we must look for ways to make ourselves, our students, our organizations, and our communities better.

PROVERB 17: *If you try to wrestle down your father, his wrapper will cover your eyes.*

UNDERLYING EDUCATIONAL PRINCIPLES

Freedom comes with responsibility. One is never too grown up to respect himself, others, and systems. Experience is critical in what educators and leaders do. It is important to respect seniority or experience in what we do. New educators and leaders must respect systemic rules and regulations. Iconoclastic notions can be counterproductive to systemic advancements. It takes individual responsibility to build group dynamics and traditions. Without personal responsibility, cultural strongholds are dislodged.

> *PROVERB #18: When you chew the dried meat, it fills up your mouth.*

UNDERLYING EDUCATIONAL PRINCIPLES

It takes personal responsibility to know your limits. You must be careful about what you do at all times. Sometimes as educators and leaders, we take on more than we can handle. We must be realistic and responsible as we bite off our problems and advance solutions. It surely takes personal responsibility to know what we can or cannot do.

PROVERB #19: *You can cry all you want, but you cannot cry out blood.*

UNDERLYING EDUCATIONAL PRINCIPLES

There is always a limit to what we can do. As a result, we must be responsible for our own actions and when to take our losses and move on. Educators and leaders must expect some forms of success and some forms of failure. However, when there is failure, we must learn from it and move on with our lives. It is self-responsible to know what to do and what the consequences of our actions will be.

PROVERB #20: Where you live is where you protect.

UNDERLYING EDUCATIONAL PRINCIPLES

Self-protection is a part of self-responsibility. It involves the ability to respect one's boundaries and deal with one's problems. Since self-protection is a life necessity, it behooves us to make our environments conducive for all. In addition, it encourages individual and group valuing that lead to maximum productivity. Self-protection involves self-pride. However, with pride comes prejudice, which can create enmity in group dynamics. As educators and leaders, we must engage in self-protection in what we do as professionals. However, we must understand that it is our duty to make opportunities available to others to enhance collaborative and consultative spirits in classrooms and organizations. In our efforts to protect our domains, we must make them conducive to others. Self-protection is important, especially when it is devoid of exclusivity.

PROVERB #21: Money is the beauty of a man.

UNDERLYING EDUCATIONAL PRINCIPLES

Typically, men are viewed as handsome and women are viewed as beautiful; and life cannot be sustained without money. Clearly, it is the responsibility of people to provide money to bring to fruition all human activities and life-sustaining programs. Money is the fuel of life. It is needed for human survival just as it is needed for programmatic stability. In other words, no human being or program can survive without money. As a result, educators and leaders need money to fund new programs to address daily or long-term human problems. However, they must adequately manage the funds as they solve problems and build programs. While money in itself cannot teach or lead, it is extremely useful in improving programs vital to students and institutions. On the other hand, the overreliance on money can cause problems and lead to nonproductive evil actions. In the end, we must view it as our human responsibility to provide and manage money for programmatic excellence.

> ## PROVERB #22: It is not the load that breaks us down; it is the way we carry it.

UNDERLYING EDUCATIONAL PRINCIPLES

How we do what we do is absolutely important. It is our responsibility to understand and value the inevitability of crises and stressors in whatever we do; however, how we manage them can create positive pathways for success. As educators and leaders, we must be cognizant of the loads that we are carrying. In addition, we must be knowledgeable about how to carry these loads. In other words, we must avoid the naïveté that presents life from a puritanical perfectionist perspective. A full life presents "all sides of the coin"—this multidimensionality highlights life's misery and beauty.

> ## *PROVERB #23: A good name shines in the dark.*

UNDERLYING EDUCATIONAL PRINCIPLES

Goodness is next to Godliness. Integrity matters; and it will continue to matter in classrooms and organizations. It is important that we understand our role in maintaining our good name. In addition, we must maintain good and uncontaminated honesty in our interactions with people different from us. Educators and leaders must maintain proper goodness in their actions and deliberations. It is truly good to be good. As educators and leaders, we must be worried about how posterity will remember us. We must keep our powders dry and be true to type. Since the goal of any program is to make it good and worthwhile, it is critical that good people direct it to achieve the desired dividend. Educators must be truly good; programs must be truly good to motivate parents to be involved in making their children good. Integrity transcends these ideals—we cannot succeed in achieving integrity unless educators and leaders with integrity are empowered.

> ## PROVERB #24: A person who does not concede defeat is not a good sport.

UNDERLYING EDUCATIONAL PRINCIPLES

Failure can have rewarding after-effects in life. It can be reha-bilitating to suffer from defeat—we learn a lot from failure and defeat. We have sometimes heard that failure is not an option. But how do we know that we are successful when we have not failed? Failure recognizes life's imperfections. When there is fail-ure in our lives, we learn from it and make sure it rarely occurs. As educators and leaders, we must concede failure and learn from it as we work with students, colleagues, and partners. Clearly, it is not how many times we are defeated, it is what we have learned after we are defeated.

> ## PROVERB #25: A person who praises the rain has been rained on.

UNDERLYING EDUCATIONAL PRINCIPLES

It is common knowledge that experience is powerful. Without experiential knowledge, there is no foundation to work with. It is self-responsible to develop knowledge. You cannot talk about anything truthfully until you have experienced and experimented on it! As educators and leaders, what we know is what we know; and it is based on this knowledge that we solve problems, set our priorities, shift our paradigms, and plan for the future. In the spiritual front, the rain washes off our sins. In other words, our knowledge of our strengths and weaknesses helps us to build our inspiration and fortitude. Education and leadership come with experience; and with experience come learning, doing, and teaching.

CHAPTER TWO

Proverbs That Teach Collaboration and Consultation

> ## PROVERB #1: *Life is in the ears.*

UNDERLYING EDUCATIONAL PRINCIPLES

Active listening is one of the basic ingredients of human communications and interactions. When we listen, we build communities. Great educators and leaders listen to students, parents, colleagues, supervisors, communities, and governments. In addition, they design programs that enhance collaboration, consultation, and cooperation.

PROVERB #2: To come and eat is not to come and work!

UNDERLYING EDUCATIONAL PRINCIPLES

It is important to know that there is time for everything, a time to celebrate and a time to work! The invitation to eat must be honored by community members. As educators, we must know the difference; there is a time to play and a time to work. Leaders must know when to reward their team members, and educators must know when to reward their students.

PROVERB #3: A tree cannot make a forest.

UNDERLYING EDUCATIONAL PRINCIPLES

A person is a part of a community and his or her interests are tied to community interests. Excellent educators and leaders must collaborate, consult, and cooperate for a system to be functional. Without teamwork and partnership, no organization can solve problems, advance its mission and vision, and maintain stability.

PROVERB #4: When mother cow is chewing grass, the younger ones look at her mouth.

UNDERLYING EDUCATIONAL PRINCIPLES

Observation is a critical learning-teaching technique. It is no surprise that observation is an important aspect of education and leadership. We must be prepared to learn from others. In other words, educators and leaders are role models who can influence how their students, colleagues, and team members behave. We teach and lead by modeling appropriate behaviors.

PROVERB #5: It takes a whole village to raise a child.

UNDERLYING EDUCATIONAL PRINCIPLES

The community must work together to solve community problems. Educators and leaders are part of a team, and they must work together in partnership to create ideas and advance the community. Individuals, institutions, professionals, community leaders, and government agencies must work as a team for the common good. Interactions are made functional and operational when everyone is a part of the team.

> **PROVERB #6:** *When you wrestle someone to the ground, you also wrestle yourself to the ground because when you stand up, he will stand up with you.*

UNDERLYING EDUCATIONAL PRINCIPLES

Problems are solved when people work together. Progressive and regressive decisions affect everyone; and how, when, and why we are involved must be clearly delineated. Educators and leaders must understand that the decisions they make have far-reaching effects on everyone. "Each One, Reach One" should be the motto of any educator and leader.

> ## PROVERB #7: *A fool does not know that his brother or sister is a visitor.*

UNDERLYING EDUCATIONAL PRINCIPLES

Because of the complexities of our daily activities, we sometimes get a little overwhelmed and forget that we are our brother's or sister's keeper. As a result, we engage in counterproductive actions (e.g., being too busy to send congratulatory notes or thank-you notes to deserving people). There is power and magic in "fluffy" actions (e.g., making positive statements, such as "good job," is needed). Educators and leaders must reward those who deserve to be rewarded—no one should be made "invisible" in the classroom or organization. Sometimes, educators and leaders take their hardworking students, staff, colleagues, or parents for granted. We ought to reward greatness and not take it for granted. To build community, we must honor community.

PROVERB #8: The fly without an advisor follows the dead body into the grave.

UNDERLYING EDUCATIONAL PRINCIPLES

The advisor and advisee are important elements in the communication realms. It is important that we engage in active listening in our personal and group interactions with others. When we turn deaf ears to advice, we lose. As a result, educators and leaders must advance their mission and vision by listening to others whose views might sometimes appear heretical. Good advice can sometimes come from unexpected quarters. It is critical for educators and leaders to listen actively.

> *PROVERB #9: A gathering of kinsmen or kinswomen is an opportunity to honor the living and the dead.*

UNDERLYING EDUCATIONAL PRINCIPLES

It is important that people gather to build a sense of community. Such community gatherings tend to be geared toward problem solving. Without a community of educators and leaders, problems will remain unresolved. As community members, we must help to build a community of peoples in our multicultural society and world.

PROVERB #10: When two elephants fight, grasses suffer.

UNDERLYING EDUCATIONAL PRINCIPLES

Whatever we do affects us and our community. Conflicts are inevitable in any system or community; and they can sometimes help to advance divergent viewpoints. However, when they go unresolved, they create immense systemic problems. Educators and leaders must avoid power struggles of any kind because they can lead to more problems and disunity in an organization. It is critical that educators and leaders engage in crisis intervention strategies that can reduce retrogressive struggles. For example, when parents blame teachers and teachers blame parents, students suffer. Similarly, when teachers blame principals and principals blame teachers, students suffer. In all cases, when adults fail to resolve their conflicts, our children suffer.

PROVERB #11: Laughter is just a matter of moving back the cheek.

UNDERLYING EDUCATIONAL PRINCIPLES

It does not cost anything to be nice to people. Similarly, it does not hurt to be a social being in any system or community. Many educators and leaders take themselves too seriously. Fluffy actions like smiling and simple acknowledgments are wonderful icebreakers in human interactions. Good educators and leaders practice fluffy actions that lead to individual valuing and community upliftment.

PROVERB #12: A good friend is better than a bad family member.

UNDERLYING EDUCATIONAL PRINCIPLES

Friendship is a human phenomenon. We know that there are people who attract our attention. Educators and leaders must continue to advance good friendships in whatever they do. They must continue to build trust in what they do. It is critical that they build good friendships and teams with others as they design collaborative and consultative ventures.

PROVERB #13: The tiger's cub does not chew grass.

UNDERLYING EDUCATIONAL PRINCIPLES

Traditionally, the young are supposed to learn from the old. To advance this thinking, experienced people must teach and mentor the neophytes, especially when they demonstrate the willingness to learn. We must learn by doing—in other words, we must experience and experiment to avoid costly mistakes and iconoclastic interpretations. Educators and leaders must observe and follow certain principles to reduce inefficiency. Good teachers are good students; and good leaders are good followers.

> *PROVERB #14: If you gave your mother counterfeit money, you actually did not spend it.*

UNDERLYING EDUCATIONAL PRINCIPLES

The family is an important part of human existence; and the mother is frequently the engine behind the family. As a result, it is unconscionable to treat a mother with disrespect and dishonor. Mothers are the glue that hold families together—when we dishonor them, we dishonor the whole family. As educators and leaders, we must cherish and value maternal/parental contributions as we build school teams and advance communities. When we lie and cheat, we betray our trust and destroy teams, organizations, and communities.

> ## PROVERB #15: The person who sits next to someone can easily smell his mouth.

UNDERLYING EDUCATIONAL PRINCIPLES

We learn about people when we work closely with them. As a result, we are forced to make fewer presumptions about them and what they value. For people to collaborate, consult, and cooperate with others, they must try to know who they are. Educators and leaders are usually successful when they know their students, clients, supporters, and detractors. The fewer assumptions we make about others, the less prejudicial we become.

PROVERB #16: The knife and the axe do not compete.

UNDERLYING EDUCATIONAL PRINCIPLES

Competition is a part of life; however, when it gets to be ruthless, it becomes counterproductive. Rather than engage in worthless competition that is devoid of common sense, it is important to engage in collaboration, consultation, and cooperation. Additionally, we must understand our limits as human beings and know when to seek help and use resource persons. As educators and leaders, we must understand that fingers are not all equal and that we perform better when we use them all.

PROVERB #17: You cannot climb a tree without support.

UNDERLYING EDUCATIONAL PRINCIPLES

Individualism is a great success-oriented attribute—it recognizes efforts and highlights resiliency and gallantry. However, it can be anticollaboration and anticommunity. Problems are frequently solved when people support and work with each other. Egocentrism and self-aggrandizement can have devastating effects on human relations and societal development. Educators and leaders must learn to give credit to others working with them. They must also rely on others in team building and consensus development. In quantifiable ways, they must encourage individual and group supports at all educational and leadership levels.

> ## PROVERB #18: Let the kite and the eagle perch and whichever one that tries to deprive the other of that right must have its wings broken.

UNDERLYING EDUCATIONAL PRINCIPLES

We all have individual spaces that should not be invaded. When we invade personal spaces, there is a likelihood that we violate people's civil rights. Yet, we must make sure that our spaces integrate and that our personal freedoms lead to the respect of other people's freedoms. Our understanding of these freedoms should motivate us to work together rather than remain apart. Our consultation, collaboration, and cooperation are crucial as our spaces and freedoms converge for the common good. As educators and leaders, we must take advantage of opportunities to work together while still respecting personal spaces, freedoms, and civil rights.

PROVERB #19: The crazy person and his mind understand.

UNDERLYING EDUCATIONAL PRINCIPLES

People differ inter-individually and intra-individually. We tend to forget that everyone, including the one who is assumed to be crazy, is different. It is important for educators and leaders to understand that they can learn from others when they are given opportunities to express themselves. Consequently, it is necessary to listen to others, get their perspectives, and see what their strengths and weaknesses are. Educators and leaders cannot afford to silence other voices, as invisible or heretical as they may be. We must take advantage of all voices, even those that sound crazy!

PROVERB #20: *In my poverty, let not poverty befall the person who might someday lend me some money.*

UNDERLYING EDUCATIONAL PRINCIPLES

One of the benefits of collaboration is consultation. With consultation comes partnership and teamwork. When we win alone, we lose alone. We increase our reservoir of goodness when we cooperate with people at all levels. In addition, we increase our wealth of experiences when we work with others. As educators and leaders, we need to build teams and friendships in what we do. As we know, "two heads are better than one"! In the end, we cannot uplift humanity without human interactions.

PROVERB #21: The child's home, even if it is trashy, is always a palace away from home.

UNDERLYING EDUCATIONAL PRINCIPLES

One of the most important elements of a child's growth is his or her home. This home depicts the kind of family that is rearing the child. In other words, the home cannot be belittled—it houses and raises the child. Sometimes, there is an underlying conflict between the school and the home. When the school does what it is supposed to do, it can become a home. This is absolutely important for children who are at risk. As educators and leaders, we must learn to work with the home and not denigrate it. In addition, we must be receptive to all students and make our school environment their home.

PROVERB #22: The rooster does not forget who plucked its feathers during the rainy season.

UNDERLYING EDUCATIONAL PRINCIPLES

Good and bad deeds are difficult to forget. But we must do good deeds so that posterity will remember us. In life, it is honorable to reach out and touch people. Educators and leaders have the power to make positive differences in the lives of others who come in contact with them. People do not really want to know what we know until they know that we care.

> *PROVERB #23: When the moon is shining, a person with a physical disability becomes hungry for a walk.*

UNDERLYING EDUCATIONAL PRINCIPLES

People get excited about different things depending on who they are, their likes and dislikes, or their responsibilities. Different people react differently to different situations. Sometimes, all they need is to be valued for who they are or for what they like or dislike. As educators and leaders, we must value their voices and try to understand, if possible, what makes them who they are. We must know why people feel the way they do, what excites them, and what makes them do what they do. Only when we value these ideals can we work with them and maximize the potential of all.

PROVERB #24: *When a child is tired of working, he resorts to fighting.*

UNDERLYING EDUCATIONAL PRINCIPLES

There is always a reason for an action. The reason can be either good or bad! It is important to find out the reason nonetheless. We cannot afford to ignore why people act the way they act. To solve a problem, we must be aware of what it is. As educators and leaders, we must acknowledge problems before we design crisis intervention strategies. For example, to solve problems of today's youth, we must do a functional behavior assessment to know antecedent behaviors. In addition, before we make behavior intervention plans, we look at all angles to discover problems and solutions. When we value and collaborate with others, we find out those secrets and solutions without making illusory generalizations.

PROVERB #25: When you dig a ditch for others, you might fall in it.

UNDERLYING EDUCATIONAL PRINCIPLES

The goal of any educational program or organization must be to maximize the fullest potential of students, teachers, parents, and communities. This goal motivates people to work together, team together, and value their differences. When people feel valued they plan for the well-being of others. When people are united, they stand together; but when they are divided, they fail together. When individuals try to pull others down, they put much weight on themselves, and thus self-destruct. As educators and leaders, we must understand that we win alone, we lose alone. Consequently, we must collaborate, consult, and cooperate to avoid antisocial nonproductive behaviors.

CHAPTER THREE

Proverbs That Teach Spirituality

> *PROVERB #1: When you eat with the devil, you must use a long spoon.*

UNDERLYING EDUCATIONAL PRINCIPLES

You must be careful about your actions and how these actions positively or negatively affect you and others. Certain individuals might be difficult to interact with, and certain environments might be conflict-ridden. As a result, it behooves educators and leaders to be creative and innovative to discover how to penetrate such individuals and communities. In addition, they must be aware of their strengths and weaknesses as they interact with others different from themselves.

> ## PROVERB #2: If you fall down and do not stand up, evil will take over.

UNDERLYING EDUCATIONAL PRINCIPLES

Failure is a part of life, but it is not the end of the road. Sometimes, people give up early when they fail in certain tasks. As educators and leaders, we must not be afraid to make mistakes—they are necessary teaching tools. Failures help us to learn how to modify who we are, what we do, and where we are going. Falling down can actually be good as long as we do not allow negativism to take over. In other words, failures can be positive when we learn from them.

PROVERB #3: *God does not give you a load that you cannot carry.*

UNDERLYING EDUCATIONAL PRINCIPLES

Spiritual powers are necessary tools for human survival. Spirituality can be used positively to teach, motivate, and build resiliency. Most religions believe in the existence, power, and kindness of God. Educators and leaders cannot afford to down-play this phenomenon in spite of their spiritual beliefs or dis-beliefs. They must understand the burdens that befall students, families, and communities; and their ability to manage conflicts must be of prime necessity.

> ## PROVERB #4: Evildoers are usually pursued by their own shadows.

UNDERLYING EDUCATIONAL PRINCIPLES

It takes energy to do good or evil. Good deeds are self-gratifying and self-rewarding; and evil deeds are shameful and self-damaging. That is why it is difficult for evil doers to go public with their actions. More often than not, they are afraid to be known and frequently masquerade their intentions. For instance, because it is evil to be racist, bigoted, and xenophobic, no educator or leader proudly admits that he or she is racist, bigoted, and xeno-phobic. Consequently, educators and leaders must acknowledge that there is good and evil in this world. However, they must encourage people to do good.

> ## PROVERB #5: Do not put yourself where your faith will fail you.

UNDERLYING EDUCATIONAL PRINCIPLES

We are the architects of our own future. We direct our faith, and in turn, our faith directs us. Individuals have different spiritual relationships with themselves and they are sometimes directed by these spiritual tendencies. As educators and leaders, we must be pure in our intentions and build our credibility by what we do. Our job is to solve problems and not create them. As a result, when we see that our actions will create problems, we must avoid them and rechannel our thinking toward positive directions. Sometimes, we abet evil deeds by our actions or inactions, and thus betray our faith.

> PROVERB #6: I am holding my staff and you are holding your staff, but the staff knows who is holding it.

UNDERLYING EDUCATIONAL PRINCIPLES

The staff is highly respected in most cultures. There is some form of spirituality that is attached to it. Certain people are supposed to have the power to carry the staff. In many societies, it defines power, hope, and faith. In other words, the holding of the staff has some spiritual connection. As educators and leaders, we must understand power, who has it, and the responsibility attached to it. Depending on the situation and circumstance, our students, parents, colleagues, and communities have power; but with this power comes responsibility. As we value our personal powers and freedoms, we must value other people's powers and freedoms. If not, our actes gratuits *collide and everybody suffers.*

PROVERB #7: The toughest head carries the masquerade.

UNDERLYING EDUCATIONAL PRINCIPLES

Not every head is a tough head. Some people are stronger than others—they do impossible things and create impressive auras. According to tradition, masquerades are connected to spirituality and they are sometimes messengers of other Supreme beings. As a result, they are supposed to do impossible things that ordinary people cannot do. As educators and leaders, we must value different strengths and weaknesses that people bring to the table. We must appreciate individual differences and understand that not everyone can teach or lead. Logically, we need truly good teachers and leaders to advance peoples and communities. Those who can, teach; and those who can, lead!

> ## PROVERB #8: Let's continue to sacrifice and let the blame go to the Gods.

UNDERLYING EDUCATIONAL PRINCIPLES

Sometimes in life, you have to do what you have to do! It is difficult to please everyone; however, we must continue to try our best. In many non-Christian environments, gods are worshipped and viewed as protectors. In some quarters, it is assumed that these gods make ways to reach the Supreme God. Clearly, there is always a supernatural being that protects everyone. This proves that we are all vulnerable in our very nature as human beings. As educators and leaders, we must continue to try our very best in whatever we do, but we must also try to be accountable as we do what we do.

PROVERB #9: God gives and God takes.

UNDERLYING EDUCATIONAL PRINCIPLES

For many people in this world, God has the power to do and undo. This religious belief goes beyond Christendom—it is connected with spirituality. As educators and leaders, we must understand the spiritual connectivities of students, colleagues, and team members. As we teach and lead, we must be careful about people's beliefs and how they affect what we do as professionals. While such beliefs can create problems in collaborative engagements, they must be respected in school and workplaces to avoid conflicts.

> ## PROVERB #10: If you are better than someone, you might be better than his God.

UNDERLYING EDUCATIONAL PRINCIPLES

In life, there are talents and gifts just as there are limits and boundaries. What we know is what we know and what we do not know is what we do not know! However, we must be careful as we acknowledge who is better and who is not. Educators and leaders must know and value people's strengths and limitations. They must also be aware of problems associated with the egocentric notion of superiority that can impinge upon collaboration, consultation, cooperation, and teamwork.

PROVERB #11: No person is God.

UNDERLYING EDUCATIONAL PRINCIPLES

In many quarters, God is a supreme and supernatural being who can do and undo. More often than not, religiosity goes hand-in-glove with spirituality. In some ways, spirituality connects itself to values that govern human actions. Even the most powerful educators and leaders are accountable to someone at some level. The understanding that we are accountable to someone, even at the spiritual level, inspires us as educators and leaders to do good, serve others, and support others who are different from us.

PROVERB #12: God knows the heart of everyone.

UNDERLYING EDUCATIONAL PRINCIPLES

Our hearts are sometimes revealed through our actions. It is no surprise that we assume that there is a Supreme and supernatural being that knows our hearts. As educators and leaders, we must understand that everyone is accountable to someone. We cannot quite predict everyone, but we can guess who they are through their actions. To a large measure, these actions can help define where their hearts are. From a religious perspective, there is a God that knows whatever we are thinking and why we do what we do. Educators and leaders cannot afford to denigrate religiosity in their efforts to teach and lead.

PROVERB #13: The same mother delivers the children, but the same God does not create them alike.

UNDERLYING EDUCATIONAL PRINCIPLES

In life, there is always a struggle between nature and nurture. While there are human attributes that are genetically based, human beings are different intra-individually and inter-individually. Brothers and sisters from the same mother and father frequently exhibit unique behavioral patterns. We must honor these differences as we make judgments about people different from us. As educators and leaders, we cannot afford to be tied to one-sided thinking when it comes to human valuing and human differences. We must cherish these differences as we teach and learn and as we interact with teachers, parents, colleagues, and partners.

PROVERB #14: When you believe, your God will believe.

UNDERLYING EDUCATIONAL PRINCIPLES

There is an intriguing joy in the self-determination that results in accurate self-knowledge, self-valuation, and self-responsibility. While some people resent confident people or people who believe in the power of the self, there is a spiritual connectivity that is attached to self-valuing. This can sometimes be tricky because without hard work, self-determination can fail to produce some desired results. As educators and leaders, we must understand the magnetic, mysterious, and magnanimous power of self-determination. It is no wonder that we are able to do some impressive unbelievable things when we believe in ourselves and others. Sometimes, we surprise our skeptical "selves" when we take charge of what we do.

PROVERB #15: God's time is the best.

UNDERLYING EDUCATIONAL PRINCIPLES

There is a limit to how far we can push our time and ourselves. When we move too fast or too slow we make mistakes. Sometimes, these mistakes can be deadly! It is important that we understand our capabilities and incapabilities. As educators and leaders, we must know why, when, and how we push time. There is a spiritual force that guides our actions and our time. It is okay to have the drive, but we must know our limitations as we drive. Sometimes it is impossible to solve every problem when we want to solve it!

> ## PROVERB #16: You can never become someone else's God.

UNDERLYING EDUCATIONAL PRINCIPLES

Power is good, but it can have a corrupting influence on people. Because of the influence of power, some people sometimes play God. Power can have a toxic influence on people to the extent that they begin to overestimate their worth and importance. The danger is that when they overestimate themselves, they underestimate others. In some ways, this behavior creates tensions in classrooms, organizations, and human interactions. As educators and leaders, we must understand that we are working with fellow humans. Our behaviors toward others influence how much we can get out of them. We cannot afford to underestimate or overestimate others.

> *PROVERB #17: The opportunity that God sends does not wake up someone who is asleep.*

UNDERLYING EDUCATIONAL PRINCIPLES

Heaven helps those who help themselves; and lazy or nonchalant people miss out on ample opportunities. Hard work is a great springboard for success. Without commitment and dedication, success is hard to find. Educators and leaders must understand that their success is dependent on what they do. Truly good teachers teach, and truly good leaders lead. They must consistently shift their paradigms and work hard to become exemplary professionals.

PROVERB #18: Everyone has his own God.

UNDERLYING EDUCATIONAL PRINCIPLES

We have our spiritual hopes and aspirations in life; and we have our likes and dislikes based on our personal idiosyncrasies. We cannot be other people—we must be ourselves and our own God's creation. In other words, we are uniquely different in and amongst ourselves. As educators and leaders, we must understand that just as we differ in all that we do, we also differ in our spiritual connectivities. As a result, we must be careful in our judgments about others.

PROVERB #19: There is no partnership between good and evil.

UNDERLYING EDUCATIONAL PRINCIPLES

In the spiritual realm, there is good and evil. Sometimes when apples and oranges are mixed up, problems arise and confusions are maximized. Knowing where we stand is necessary to prevent wishy-washy ideas that cause distress in human and organizational interactions. As educators and leaders, we must make good judgments and be honorable as teachers and leaders. We must also be careful about our assessment of what is good or evil. When we jump to conclusions without critical analyses, we make mistakes that have far-reaching consequences in our lives and those of others.

PROVERB #20: A person who ridicules good will become overtaken by evil.

UNDERLYING EDUCATIONAL PRINCIPLES

In life, there are people who refuse to honor goodness in quality people, situations, and events. They are usually skeptics who derive pleasure in the blame game or in seeing people sad. They see no good and do lots of evil! But then, there are others who believe in the goodness of the human spirit. These individuals take advantage of the human gifts and talents, recognize different personal and group strengths, and develop the human capital needed to build people and organizations. Educators and leaders must recognize good individuals as they work with students and teams of people. Additionally, they must become good individuals if they create environments where good individuals thrive. On the whole, we must avoid the crab-bucket syndrome (i.e., the tendency to drag people down because they are better than us) in order to uplift our students and teams.

PROVERB #21: *The fear of God is not based on what we wear.*

UNDERLYING EDUCATIONAL PRINCIPLES

In Christendom, there is the belief that God is everywhere. Most people believe that there is some supernatural force more powerful than us. People respond to spiritual connections based on their fundamental beliefs. However, the tragedy is that belief systems struggle over what is or what is not. As a result, the argument comes down to the level of who will go to heaven or hell; who God loves or hates; or who is more spiritual or puritanical than the other. Not surprisingly, we sometimes demonstrate our faith based on how we dress and not based on what we do. As educators and leaders, our actions must be louder than our words. In the end, we must honor results and not emotions.

PROVERB #22: A person who trusts in God lacks nothing.

UNDERLYING EDUCATIONAL PRINCIPLES

On the U.S. dollar bill, we see the statement, In God We Trust. Everyone uses this dollar bill to buy and sell. All over the world, this trust in God translates to human valuing. When we value others, we respect and listen to their voices. Logically, these voices are created by God. As educators and leaders, we must know that some of our students and colleagues value God as the creator of all humans. To connect with them, we must trust God's works in all of us. If we believe He has some power, we must believe He inspires us to do "good" toward others, our religiosity notwithstanding.

PROVERB #23: *A witch doctor does not cure himself.*

UNDERLYING EDUCATIONAL PRINCIPLES

This statement justifies the belief that we must learn from others in life. Witch doctors are specialists in their crafts; but from time to time, they need the collaboration, consultation, and cooperation of other professionals. Though there is a spiritual overtone to this statement, we must rely on others as needed. Educators and leaders must master their craft; however, they must collaborate, consult, and cooperate in all their activities. This humble awareness sets the stage for paradigm shift, innovative problem-solving, and individual well-being. We win alone, and we lose alone! Teamwork and partnership must be encouraged in our classrooms and organizations.

> ## PROVERB #24: Where there are many people, there God is.

UNDERLYING EDUCATIONAL PRINCIPLES

This spiritual statement is connected to the mysterious nature of God, and to a large measure, depicts the goodness that exists between and within human beings. Ironically, in human interactions, there are people who refuse to manifest this goodness or beauty in building and sustaining individuals and communities. As educators and leaders, we must understand, value, and use the goodness that students and colleagues bring to the table. We must believe in this goodness as we collaborate, consult, and cooperate with others different from us.

PROVERB #25: *The veil spirit of a person is a person.*

UNDERLYING EDUCATIONAL PRINCIPLES

We frequently play the blame game in whatever we do. We attribute our failures to others and selfishly attribute our successes to ourselves. There are good and evil people; and we tend to forget that we are the architects of our own futures. As educators and leaders, we must work hard to redeem ourselves by our good deeds and actions. We must live by examples and try to model appropriate behaviors for our future generations. While it is tempting for us to abuse our powers, it is our ultimate responsibility to keep our powders dry. We are who we are, but we can make ourselves better human beings so that posterity will remember us. Not only do we have roles to play in making our lives better, we have roles to play in making other people's lives better. In our classrooms and workplaces, we can create the wonderful spirit of goodwill toward others. Rather than curse our darkness, we must try to light the candles in all of us.

CHAPTER FOUR

Proverbs That Teach Other Life Lessons

PROVERB #1: Nights have ears.

UNDERLYING EDUCATIONAL PRINCIPLES

Since nights are dark, visibility is difficult. Logically, this makes it difficult to see, but makes it easier to hear. As a result, one must talk with caution and intelligence. Secrets have ways of unveiling themselves. As educators and leaders, we must know who we talk to, when we talk, and why we talk. In addition, we must be aware that people interpret what they hear differently based on their likes and dislikes. Depending on situations, this can create or solve problems.

CR ED

PROVERB #2: As much as you love your husband, you will not want to be buried alive with him.

UNDERLYING EDUCATIONAL PRINCIPLES

No person is bigger than an organization, and people come and go, but systems continue to exist and even advance. Educators and leaders must know that it is required of them to be prudent in decision making and team building. Clearly, they must endeavor to make sense of the following African fable:

Once upon a time, there was a woman who was so in love with her husband that when he died she wanted to be buried alive with him. Everyone begged her not to do that, but she refused! As a result, the elders met and decided to solve this dilemma. As they were putting the man's coffin in the grave, the woman jumped in, and they decided to bury her along with her husband as she had requested. Oddly enough, she then pleaded with the people to let her out of the grave. She wanted to live! In fact, she proved that common sense is a powerful force in life.

CR ED

> *PROVERB #3: When a poor person is told what it takes to be rich, he might prefer to remain poor.*

UNDERLYING EDUCATIONAL PRINCIPLES

It is always important to speak the truth; however, the truth can be scary to hear sometimes. There is a big difference between fact and fiction. Good educators must look for innovative ways to confront reality; and good leaders must be tactful and empathetic on how they tell the truth. The goal must be to motivate and not to discourage!

PROVERB #4: *The frog does not come out in the daytime for nothing.*

UNDERLYING EDUCATIONAL PRINCIPLES

Nothing happens without reason—that reason might be right or wrong! It is no surprise that educators and leaders are guided by certain goals and objectives. As a consequence, it is important for educators and leaders to authenticate their goals and objectives through legitimate actions. In fact, they must be prepared to account for the reasons for their actions.

> ## PROVERB #5: A traveler is more knowledgeable than an aged person.

UNDERLYING EDUCATIONAL PRINCIPLES

A traveler experiences new situations because of the vulnerability that is connected to traveling. He or she sees new things, learns new ideas, and shifts paradigms and powers. That is why attending workshops, symposia, and conferences is a part of what educators and leaders do. Good educators and leaders travel to learn and disseminate new ideas and new ways of thinking.

PROVERB #6: The dying dog does not smell the bad odor.

UNDERLYING EDUCATIONAL PRINCIPLES

When emotions rule, people misbehave and become desperate and dangerous. We must be cautious about the herd mentality that forces people to refuse to reason. Educators and leaders must be careful about pushing themselves and others to the wall. When people feel frustrated, they engage in self-destructive behaviors that lead to infinite failure.

PROVERB #7: We never go back to yesterday.

UNDERLYING EDUCATIONAL PRINCIPLES

Events happen! Sometimes, they are good, sometimes bad; and we tend to remember them as they have affected us. However, we want to know when to stop belaboring the past. Educators and leaders must learn to use the past to deal with the present and predict the future. They must be progressive in their thinking as they resolve existing conflicts. They cannot afford to dwell in the past even when the past is beautiful or ugly.

PROVERB #8: Patience is king.

UNDERLYING EDUCATIONAL PRINCIPLES

Patience is a wonderful virtue that everyone should adopt. We must be careful about running with our emotions. As educators and leaders, we need to be much more careful and patient in our dealings with people. Our patience can reduce our stressors and negative judgments and increase our ability to manage conflicts. Educators and leaders must realize that the search for instant gratification can lead to improper planning, poor judgments, and illusory generalizations.

*PROVERB #9: You do not
tell a deaf person that a crowd is
gathering at the market square.*

UNDERLYING EDUCATIONAL PRINCIPLES

Deaf people can hear, but they can hear through other senses. Deafness has nothing to do with one's intelligence, resiliency, and survival skills. There is a tendency to downplay the senses that people bring to the table. As educators and leaders, we must begin to respect the intellectual and sensory packages that others have. People can see what we do and sense whether we are with them or against them.

PROVERB #10: The hot soup is usually licked slowly.

UNDERLYING EDUCATIONAL PRINCIPLES

We have frequently wondered why people are always in a hurry. Hurrying prevents mastery and increases inefficiency. Educators and leaders must be careful about not rushing into decisions without thorough preparation. They must be vigilant about not rushing into judgments and allowing their emotions to run wild. In addition, they must continue to be patient and careful because the decisions they make might have far-reaching consequences on others.

PROVERB #11: When the wind blows, you see the chicken's buttocks.

UNDERLYING EDUCATIONAL PRINCIPLES

One situation leads to another; and each can reveal a lot when it happens. There are actions and reactions in life; and we learn from them. Disruptions of any kind affect what we do with ourselves, our students, colleagues, organizations, and communities. As educators and leaders, we must be careful about how we handle situations, intervene in crises, manage stressors, and build teams. Our inability to perform these actions will expose us in negative lights and bring ridicule to our organizations.

PROVERB #12: Truth is life.

UNDERLYING EDUCATIONAL PRINCIPLES

Truth brings honor to people, organizations, and communities. It unveils realities—though they can build communities, they can create problems. One of the infinite goals in life is to be truthful to yourself and others. Educators and leaders must endeavor to tell the truth all the time. Truths add realities to what we do in our classrooms and jobs. Without truths, programs and people lose their integrity.

PROVERB #13: Soiled hands lead to the oily mouth.

UNDERLYING EDUCATIONAL PRINCIPLES

Hard work, dedication, and commitment yield fruitful dividends. We cannot succeed in measurable ways without efforts and struggles. Committed educators and leaders frequently make quantifiable differences in the lives of their students, cohorts, colleagues, and organizations. Success and change do not just come; they come as a result of discipline, dedication, commitment, and hard work.

PROVERB #14: The patient person eats the best part of the fish.

UNDERLYING EDUCATIONAL PRINCIPLES

Patience is a wonderful virtue. It gives you time to think before you act; and it creates opportunities for planning and preparation. Clearly, prior planning prevents poor performance (i.e., the 5 P's). Educators and leaders must not rush into emotional judgments and illusory conclusions. They must think before they act, and they must be prudent in their actions. Understandably, they cannot resolve classroom, organizational, and community problems unless they patiently plan their crisis intervention strategies.

> ## PROVERB #15: All lizards are lying on their stomachs, and no one knows the one with a stomachache.

UNDERLYING EDUCATIONAL PRINCIPLES

It is difficult to make accurate assumptions about what we do not know. Clearly, what we do not know, we do not know! As a result, we must value individual differences—that is, we must know the differences between and within us. Looks can be deceiving, and it is naive to use simple answers for complex problems. As educators and leaders, we must go beyond presumptions to know realities—we make unwarranted errors when we make unwarranted generalizations about people, situations, and events. That is why what we do as professionals must be data-driven and evidence-based.

PROVERB #16: When the child's sore is healed, he tends to forget the pain.

UNDERLYING EDUCATIONAL PRINCIPLES

History is a part of our lives; and when we forget it, we forget our past and find it difficult to predict our future. While we cannot be slaves to our past, we must remember our struggles to help us to avoid repeating past mistakes. As educators and leaders, we must acknowledge and respect our tradition as we shift our paradigms. Clearly, our world is changing and growing and it is important that we grow with it. However, we do ourselves great disservice when we fail to acknowledge how we got to where we are.

PROVERB #17: A child must crawl before walking.

UNDERLYING EDUCATIONAL PRINCIPLES

Tradition and history are a part of life; and we must respect them. We tend to be in a hurry in all our activities, and as a result, we make many unpardonable mistakes. It is important that educators and leaders acknowledge that life is a stage. We must be thoughtful as we change systems and shift paradigms. As we grow, we go from stage to stage and from idea to idea. As educators and leaders, we cannot afford to be iconoclasts who have little patience for tradition. It is no surprise that we must pretest ideas before we make them systemic. We must be patient as our ideas percolate and advance to stability.

PROVERB #18: The look of a child determines if you will take food from him.

UNDERLYING EDUCATIONAL PRINCIPLES

In life, we are attracted to beauty. While this beauty is in the eyes of the beholder, we tend to fall in love with it. It is no surprise that it influences how we value what we value. Initial impressions matter! Though it is dangerous to make summations based on first impressions, it is human nature to make such summations as prejudicial as they might appear. Educators and leaders must understand that first impressions (as wrong as they might appear) can influence decisions. As a consequence, we must always be at our very best as we educate our students and lead our colleagues to a new direction.

> ## PROVERB #19: *It does not matter how bad the yam is; it is still better than the cocoyam.*

UNDERLYING EDUCATIONAL PRINCIPLES

It is important to know the difference between good and bad or what is appropriate or inappropriate. Quality must be honored in all that we do. When we downplay quality, we flounder in mediocrity. We cannot afford to be wishy-washy about this! As educators and leaders, we must acknowledge and reward quality even in our efforts to value equity. Some students and workers are just excellent in what they do, and we must acknowledge and value them.

PROVERB #20: When dried bones are mentioned, old people feel uneasy.

UNDERLYING EDUCATIONAL PRINCIPLES

Even though it is ideal to tell the truth, it still hurts and can cause some uneasiness in human interactions. As a result, we must be prudent in whatever we do. Sometimes, the truth is difficult to take! As educators and leaders, we must exercise wisdom in what we do. If our goal is to build trusting and progressive communities, we must tell the truth, but we must tell it in a tactful manner. Words can have far-reaching impacts on others.

> ## PROVERB #21: A person who is already on the floor does not need to fear a fall.

UNDERLYING EDUCATIONAL PRINCIPLES

When you are down, you are down! You build self-determination by knowing your strengths and limitations, but it can be depressing when you harp on your limitations alone. As educators and leaders, we must understand the extent of people's frustrations and limitations. However, this understanding should not be an alibi for retrogressive actions. Being down can be a situational life event, but not fearing a fall can be productive or destructive depending on the circumstance.

> ## PROVERB #22: Tomorrow is pregnant; no one knows what it might deliver.

UNDERLYING EDUCATIONAL PRINCIPLES

We are supposed to plan for the future even when we cannot easily predict it. There is some mystery about the future; that makes it intriguing in designing programs. The unpredictability of the future creates room for adaptations and modifications at the personal and organizational levels. As a result, educators and leaders must be ready to provide different, supplementary, and additional opportunities for students, organizations, institutions, and communities.

PROVERB #23: There is no use for a dry porridge.

UNDERLYING EDUCATIONAL PRINCIPLES

In realistic terms, a porridge is supposed to be watery with all kinds of tasty ingredients. When it is dry, it is no longer a porridge. As educators and leaders, our question should be, Of what use is a dry porridge? This illustrates that there is a limit to what we can do as humans. Clearly, we cannot produce what is lost. We must be aware of our limitations as teachers and leaders and know when to take our losses and move on!

PROVERB #24: As the cow gets older, its nostrils get bigger.

UNDERLYING EDUCATIONAL PRINCIPLES

The more experienced we get, the more we increase our perceptual skills! These skills help us to make fewer mistakes in judgments. There is, however, a danger in basing everything we do on past experiences—we tend to condition ourselves to what will be or what will not be. As a result, we close our eyes to new experiences when they fail to fit into prior experiences. Educators and leaders must understand that experience matters; however, they must be careful about making too much of their experiential skills.

PROVERB #25: Anything with a beginning must have an end.

UNDERLYING EDUCATIONAL PRINCIPLES

Life has a beginning and an end; and so does everything we do in life. It is critical that we value time but not become slaves to it. As educators and leaders, we must sometimes respect natural law, which stipulates that what will be, will be! We must respond to changes and the unpredictability of events. In addition, we must know that some truths are inevitable (e.g., death is an inevitable event). Clearly, educators and leaders must engage in prudent planning. For example, goals must be set and there must be a timeline to achieve them. We want problems to be solved; we do not want them to linger on. At some point in life, we must take our glories or losses and move on.

Afterword

The complicated nature of contemporary society often causes us to forget or overlook the fact that simple truths are all around us, and that they can help us find the path that we seek—to understanding, harmony, or inner peace. Each of us, no doubt, will find inspiration in reading Professor Festus Obiakor's book, *100 Multicultural Proverbs: Inspirational Affirmations for Educators.* Through this book, we are reminded that the important lessons of life are being communicated to us every day, but our minds and hearts must be open to gain the most from our observations.

All of us who profess to be educators and leaders realize that we become successful when learning, teaching, and leading actually take place. Our positions as educators and leaders often cause us to presume that the information we have chosen to bestow upon our audience carries both interest and value. We presume that people will absorb the meaning and significance of our lessons—that their intellects will be expanded and their horizons broadened. If this magical connection is not made, then surely the fault must be theirs, for it could not possibly be ours. In reality, learning, teaching, and leading must become our personal responsibilities.

Sometimes, we forget that people learn in different ways, by different means, and through different modes, and that the most effective means of teaching—and consequently the most effective learning— often results not from teaching methods that are complex, but indeed from those that are quite basic. In other words, meanings can be conveyed through a variety of approaches. Clearly, *100 Multicultural Proverbs* is a book that motivates us to provide instruction in the most fundamental terms, and in ways that are simultaneously informational and inspirational.

Through the provision of *100 Multicultural Proverbs,* Professor Obiakor effectively reminds us that knowledge and insight transcend race, culture, language, religion, and nationality. It is useful for us to frequently acknowledge the veracity of this simple statement, for all too often, we attribute insight and understanding exclusively to our own group, clan, or tribe. Professor Obiakor's interpretations of the proverbs challenge the ordinary mind to shift paradigms and power and expand our imaginations to use real principles to solve real problems. In addition, his interpretations uniquely touch on all facets of life and challenge educators and leaders to do the *right things*.

Finally, *100 Multicultural Proverbs* urges all of us to step back from time to time and consider the values and messages that we desire to transmit. It also convinces us that our focus must be on positive change, the kind of change we must become in order to learn, teach, and lead futuristically. This book clearly shows why proverbs endure across the lines of time and geography—because proverbs point us toward the truth, and the truth, as we all know, is eternal.

William B. Harvey
Vice President for Equity & Diversity Affairs
University of Virginia

CORWIN PRESS

The Corwin Press logo—a raven striding across an open book—represents the union of courage and learning. Corwin Press is committed to improving education for all learners by publishing books and other professional development resources for those serving the field of PreK–12 education. By providing practical, hands-on materials, Corwin Press continues to carry out the promise of its motto: **"Helping Educators Do Their Work Better."**